A first book of lullabies from around the world

Moondrops

For our children

Kathryn, Jessica, Erin, Paul, Joseph,

Paulingo, Kristiaan and Thomas

May they sing these lullabies to our grandchildren.

H.P., M.L. & K.O'M.

Published by Longmeadow Press
201 High Ridge Road
Stamford, CT 06904

Text copyright © 1993 Kevin O'Mara and Mark Leehy
Illustrations copyright © 1993 Heather Philpott
Designed by Patricia Tsiatsias

All rights reserved. No part of this book may be reproduced
or utilized in any form or by any means, electronic or mechanical,
including photocopying, recording or by any information storage
and retrieval system, without permission in writing from the
Publisher. Longmeadow Press and the colophon
are registered trademarks.

Printed in China by Global Com Pte Ltd

Library of Congress Cataloging-in-Publication Data

Moondrops: a first book of lullabies from around the world
illustrated by Heather Philpott; adapted by Mark Leehy and Kevin O'Mara.
p. of music.
Unacc. melodies; includes chord symbols.
Each song with English words or an English translation; includes original languages.
Originally published: Carlton, Victoria: Moondrake Australia, 1993.
ISBN 0-681-00732-X.

1. Lullabies. [1. Lullabies. 2. Songs.] I. Philpott, Heather, ill.
II. Leehy, Mark. III. O'Mara, Kevin.
M1997.M8525 1994
94-7843
CIP
AC M

First Longmeadow Press edition, 1995

0 9 8 7 6 5 4 3 2 1

A first book of lullabies from around the world

Moondrops

Illustrated by
Heather Philpott
Adapted by
Mark Leehy and Kevin O'Mara

LONGMEADOW PRESS

Acknowledgements

Our thanks to libraries everywhere, especially the gracious people at Eltham Library, Victoria. Also thanks to our friends from many lands who sang for us the songs of their childhood.

These include:

Yumiko Campbell, Ewa Czlonka, Hania Czlonka, Jan Dekker, Rob Fairbarin, Tulip Hura, Ziggy Jackson, Helmut Lopaczuk, Vince Marino, Antonietta Martin, June Nichols, Olga Pavlinov, Heather Philpott-Rehder, Tom Poata, Laura Quaremba, Greg Rough, Faye Ryan, Alex Skovron and Pam Sheldrake.

Music typeset by Fact 'n' Fictionary, Monbulk, Victoria.

All arrangements and adaptations of English words, translations and new English lyrics and adaptations of all songs appearing in this book are copyright © 1992 Mark Leehy and Kevin O'Mara.

Every care has been taken to trace and acknowledge copyright holders. The publishers apologise for any accidental infringement where copyright has been untraceable and if notified, would be pleased to rectify this in their next edition.

List of Lullabies

6   Brahms Lullaby
German

9   Kumbayah
West Indian

10   Twinkle, Twinkle, Little Star
English

13   Nursemaid's Lullaby
Japanese

14   Hush, Little Baby
American (North Carolina)

17   Au Clair de la Lune
French

18   Ninna Nanna
Italian

20   All the Pretty Little Horses
The American South

22   Hine E Hine
New Zealand (Maori)

25   Sleep, O Babe
Irish

26   Hush-a-bye Baby
English

29   Bayushka Baio
Russian

30   Starlight, Starbright
English

33   All Through the Night
Welsh

34   Golden Slumbers
English

37   Wee Willie Winkie
Scottish

38   Cradle Song
German

41   When the Night-time Comes
Polish

42   Bye, Baby Bunting
English

45   Maranoa Lullaby
Australian (Aboriginal)

46   Sleep, Baby, Sleep
Dutch

49   Lullaby My Baby
Spanish

50   Baloo Baleerie
Scottish

52   Information about the lullabies

Brahms Lullaby
German

Lullaby and goodnight,
My own little baby,
Snuggle softly and deep
In the wrappings of sleep.
When the morning shall break,
May God kiss you awake;
When the morning shall break,
May God kiss you awake.

Go to sleep and goodnight,
My own little baby,
With the moon overhead
Snuggle deep in your bed.
Close your eyes now and rest,
May these hours be blest;
Go to sleep now and rest,
May these hours be blest.

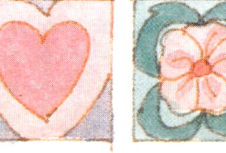

Kumbayah
West Indian

Kumbayah, my Lord, kumbayah.
Kumbayah, my Lord, kumbayah.
Kumbayah, my Lord, kumbayah.
O Lord, kumbayah,
O Lord, kumbayah.

Someone's crying, Lord, kumbayah,
O Lord, kumbayah.

Someone's singing, Lord, kumbayah,
O Lord, kumbayah.

Someone's praying, Lord, kumbayah,
O Lord, kumbayah.

Someone's sleeping, Lord, kumbayah,
O Lord, kumbayah.

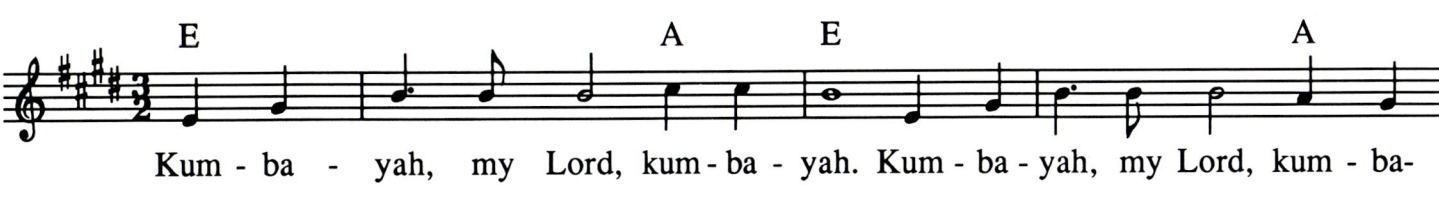
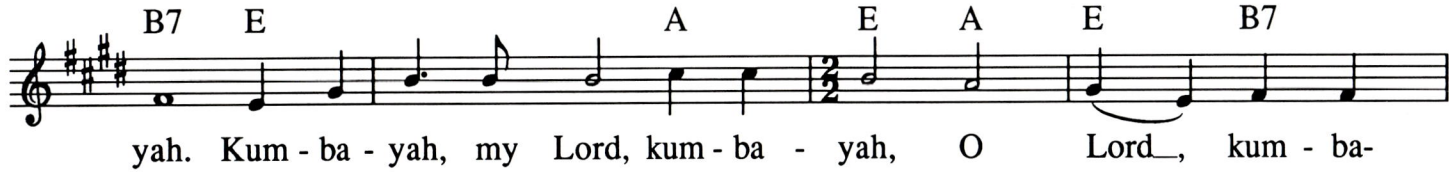
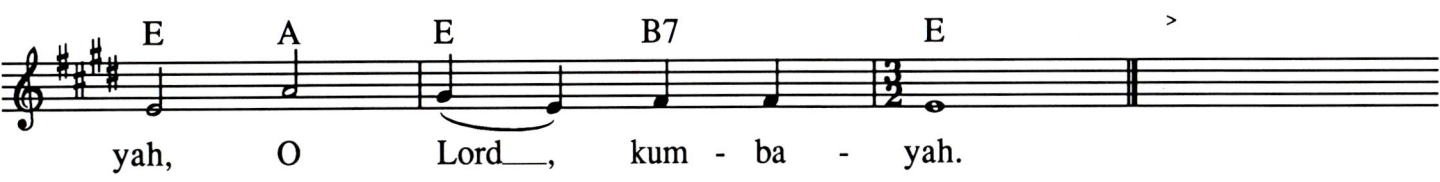

Twinkle, Twinkle, Little Star
English

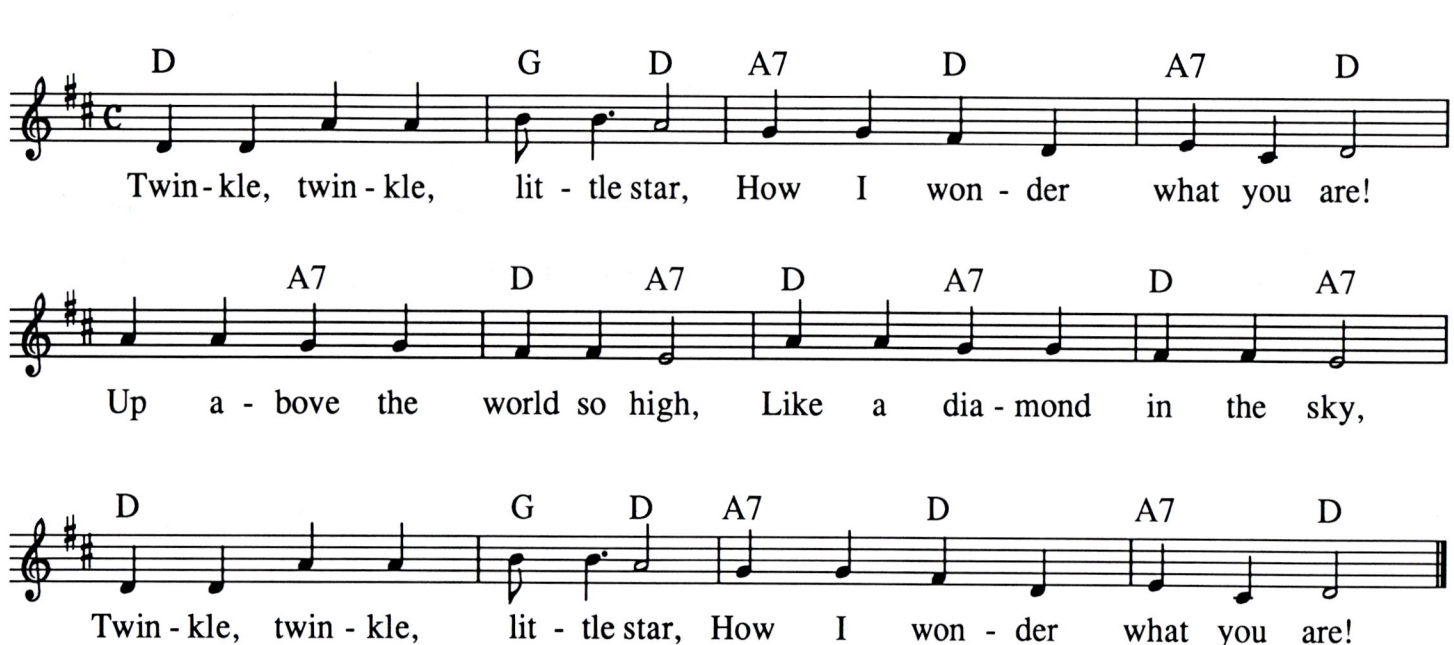

Twinkle, twinkle, little star,
How I wonder what you are!
Up above the world so high,
Like a diamond in the sky,
Twinkle, twinkle, little star,
How I wonder what you are!

In the dark blue sky you keep
And often through my curtain peep,
For you never shut your eye,
Till the sun is in the sky,
Twinkle, twinkle, little star,
How I wonder what you are!

As your bright and tiny spark
Lights the traveller in the dark,
Though I know not what you are,
Twinkle, twinkle, little star,
Twinkle, twinkle, little star,
How I wonder what you are!

Nursemaid's Lullaby
Japanese

Sleepy baby, Oh little boy,
May you sleep so well,
Many stories, little baby,
All your dreams will tell.

Where has she gone, Oh little boy?
She is far away,
Over mountains, little baby,
She has gone to play.

What presents, Oh little boy,
Did she leave for you?
Den-den drum for little baby,
A flute of bamboo?

ねんねん ころりよ
おころりよ
ぼうやは よいこだ
ねんねしな

ぼうやの おもりは
どこへ いった
あの やま こえて
さとへ いった

さとの みやげに
なに もらった
でんでんだいこに
しょうの ふえ

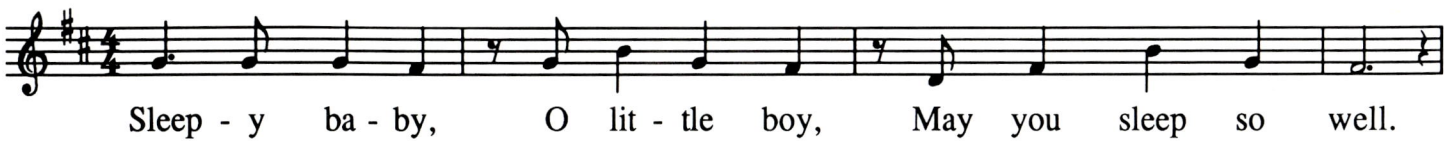

Hush, Little Baby
American (North Carolina)

Hush, little baby, don't say a word,
Papa's gonna buy you a mockingbird.

If that mockingbird won't sing,
Papa's gonna buy you a diamond ring.

And if that diamond ring turns brass,
Papa's gonna buy you a looking-glass.

And if that looking-glass get broke,
Papa's gonna buy you a billy-goat.

And if that billy-goat won't pull,
Papa's gonna buy you a cart and bull.

And if that cart and bull turn over,
Papa's gonna buy you a dog named Rover.

And if that dog named Rover won't bark,
Papa's gonna buy you a horse and cart.

And if that horse and cart fall down,
You'll still be the sweetest little child in town.

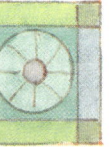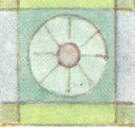

Au Clair de la Lune
French

In the silver moonlight, tapping at your door,
I have come, good neighbour, twenty miles or more;
Burnt out is my candle and it shines no more,
Open now, good neighbour, please unlock the door.

Au clair de la lune, mon ami Pierrot,
Prête-moi ta plume, pour écrire un mot;
Ma chandelle est morte, je n'ai plus de feu,
Ouvre-moi ta porte, pour l'amour de Dieu.

Ninna Nanna
Italian

Ninna nanna, lullaby,
Mother's little precious one.

Golden dreams my little dear,
Mother's heart will hold you near.

Close your eyes and listen to
The angels as they carry you,
Ninna nanna, lullaby,
Little love of mine.

Ninna nanna, ninna nanna,
Bel bambino della mamma.

Sogni d'oro piccolo amor,
Dormi, rosa sul mio cuor.

Chiudi gli occhi, ascolta,
Gli angioletti, dormi, sogna,
Ninna nanna, ninna nanna,
Piccolo amor.

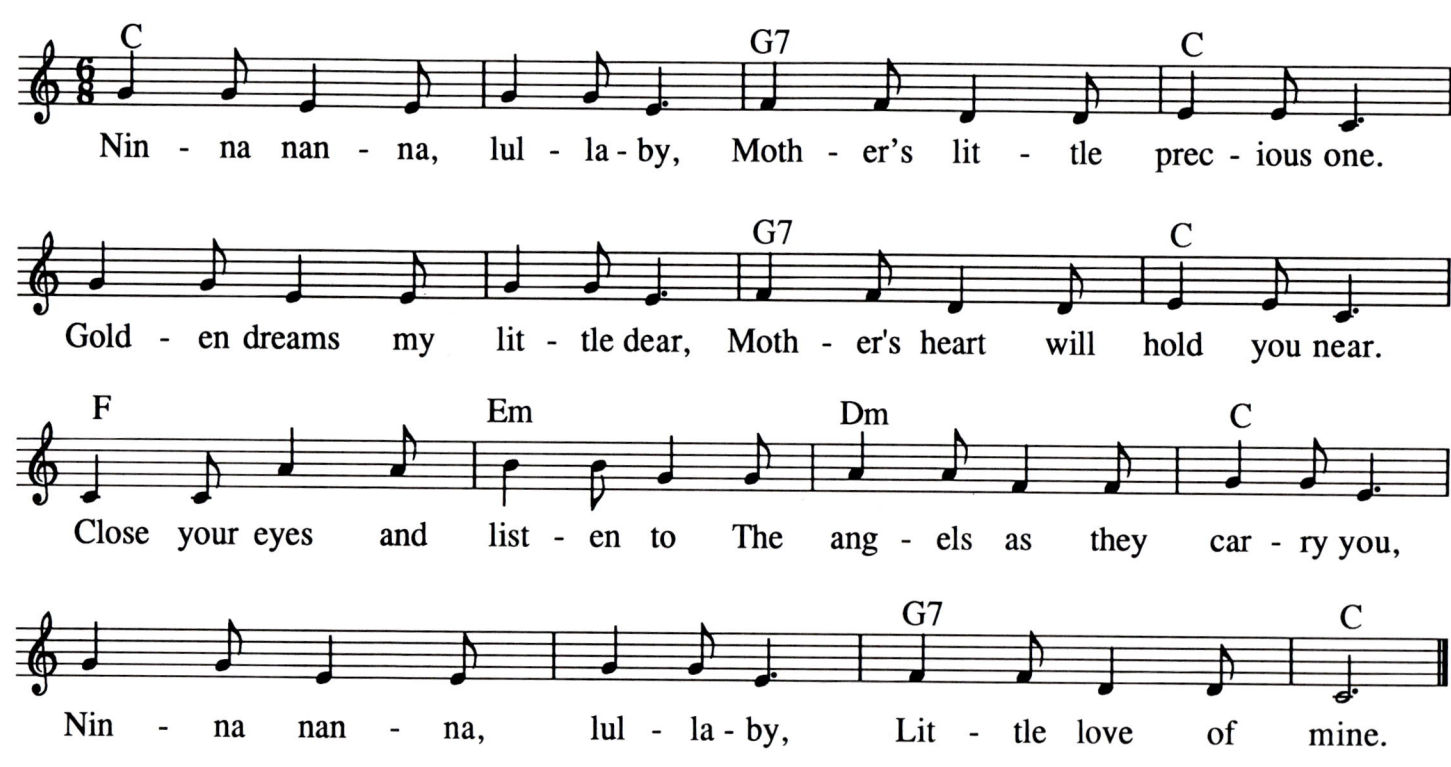

All the Pretty Little Horses
The American South

Hush-a-bye, don't you cry,
Go to sleepy little baby.
When you wake you shall take
All the pretty little horses.
Blacks and bays, dapples and grays,
Coach and six-a little horses.
Hush-a-bye, don't you cry,
Go to sleep little baby.

Hush-a-bye, don't you cry,
Go to sleepy little baby.
Mammy's here, have no fear,
Here to watch her little baby.
Sleep and rest, Mammy's blest,
Mammy's blessed little baby.
Hush-a-bye, don't you cry,
Go to sleep little baby.

Hush a bye, don't you cry, Go to sleep-y lit-tle ba-by.

When you wake you shall take All the pret-ty lit-tle hors-es.

Blacks and bays, dap-ples and grays, Coach and six-a lit-tle hors-es.

Hush a bye, don't you cry, Go to sleep-y lit-tle ba-by.

Hine E Hine
New Zealand (Maori)

Tears in your eyes, little lady,	E tangi ana koe,
Hine E Hine;	Hine E Hine;
Hush now, my tired little baby,	Kua ngenge ana koe,
Hine E Hine.	Hine E Hine.
Stars are shining above	Kati to pouri ra
Bright in the great southern sky,	Noho i te aroha,
Bright as a new father's love,	Te ngakau o te matua,
Hine E Hine,	Hine E Hine,
Hine E Hine.	Hine E Hine.

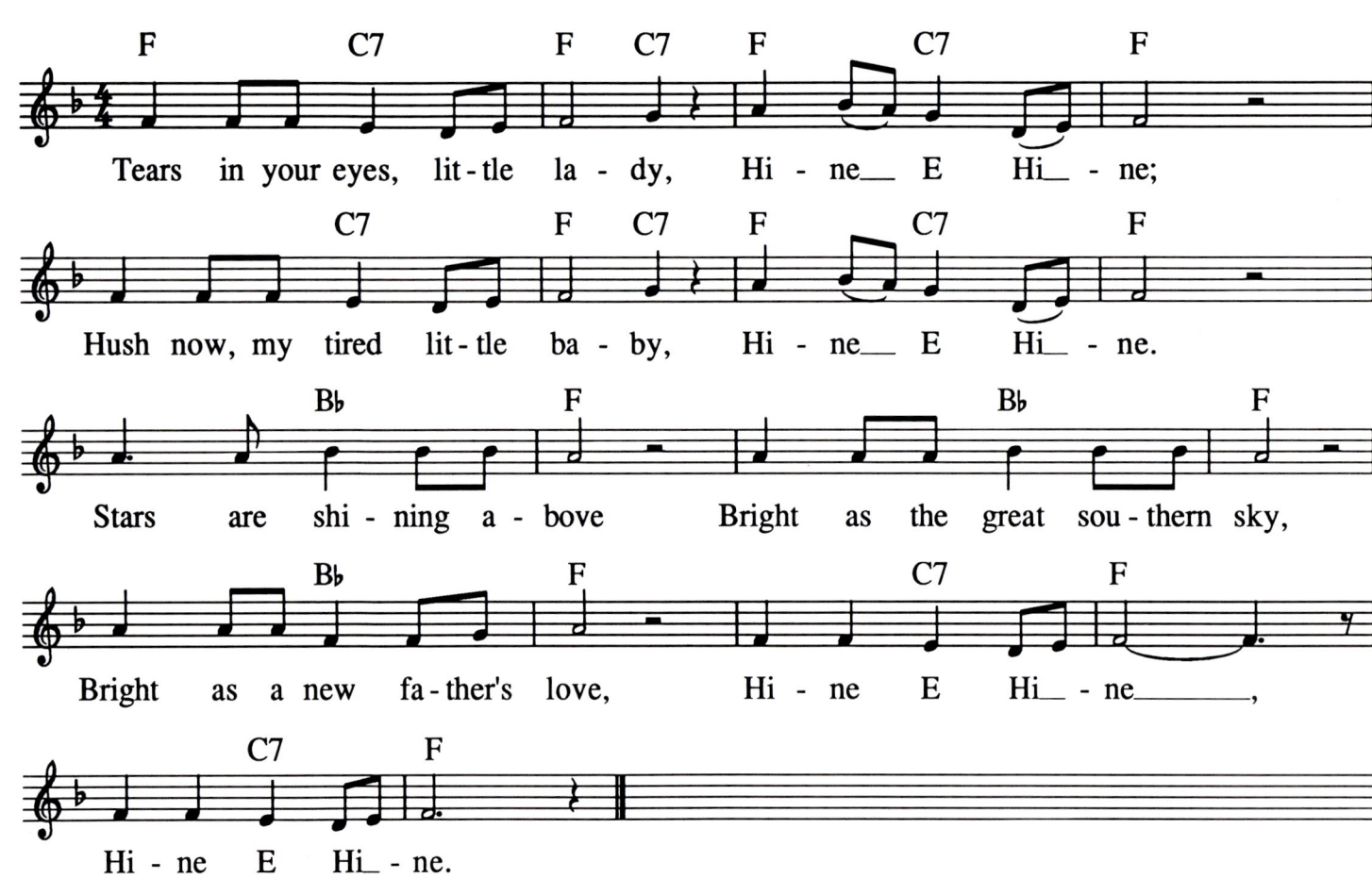

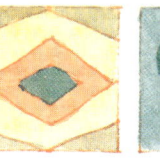

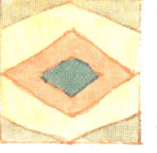

Sleep, O Babe
Irish

Sleep, O Babe, for the red bee hums
The silent twilight's fall;
Spirits from the Grey Rock come
To wrap the world in thrall.
I'll envy you, my child, my joy,
My loving heart's desire,
The crickets sing a lullaby
Beside the dying fire,
Beside the dying fire.

Dusk is drawn and the grain man's barn
Is wreathed in rings of fog;
Siobhra sails his boat till morn
Upon the starry bog.
I'll stay with you till the fading moon
Has ringed the dawn with dew,
And weeps to hear this lullaby,
I sing my love to you
I sing my love to you.

Hush-a-bye, Baby
English

Hush-a-bye, baby, on the tree top,
When the wind blows, the cradle will rock.
When the bough breaks, the cradle will fall,
And down will come baby, cradle and all.

Hush-a-bye, baby, on the tree top,
When the wind blows, the cradle will rock.
When the bough breaks, the cradle will fall,
And down will come baby, cradle and all.

Bayushka Baio
Russian

Sleep my lovely darling baby,
Bayushka Baio.
Shines the moon upon your cradle,
Bayushka Baio.

I will sing to you a song of
Stories that I know,
Close your little eyes and slumber,
Bayushka Baio.

Спи младенец мой прекрасный,
Бающки-баю.
Тихо смотрит месяц ясный
В колыбель твою.

Стану сказывать я сказки,
Песенку спою;
Ты ж дремли, закрывши глазки,
Баюшки-баю.

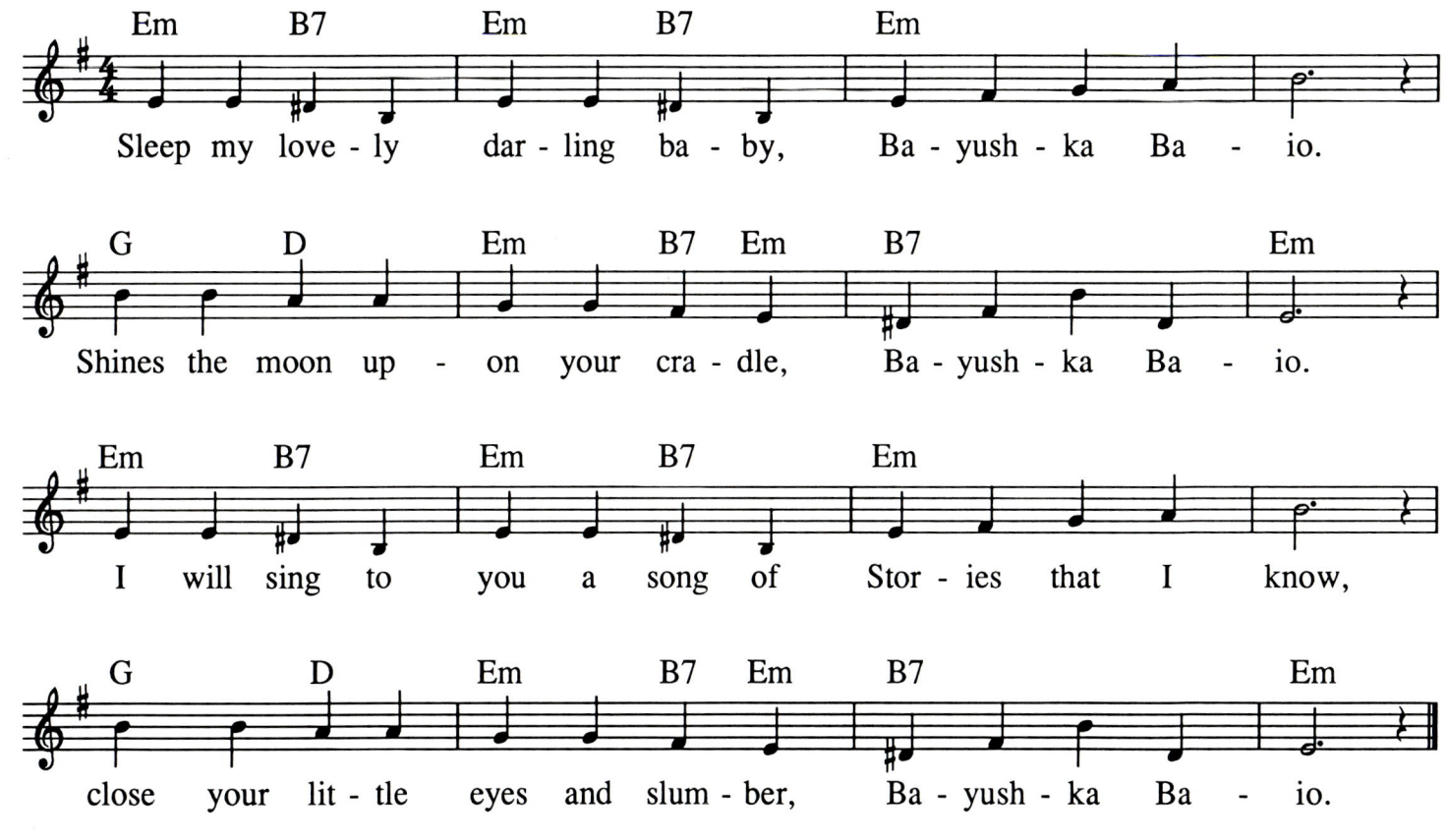

Starlight, Starbright
English

Starlight, Starbright
First star I see tonight,
Wish I may, wish I might,
Have the wish I wish tonight.

Starlight, Starbright
First star I see tonight,
Wish I may, wish I might,
Have the wish I wish tonight.

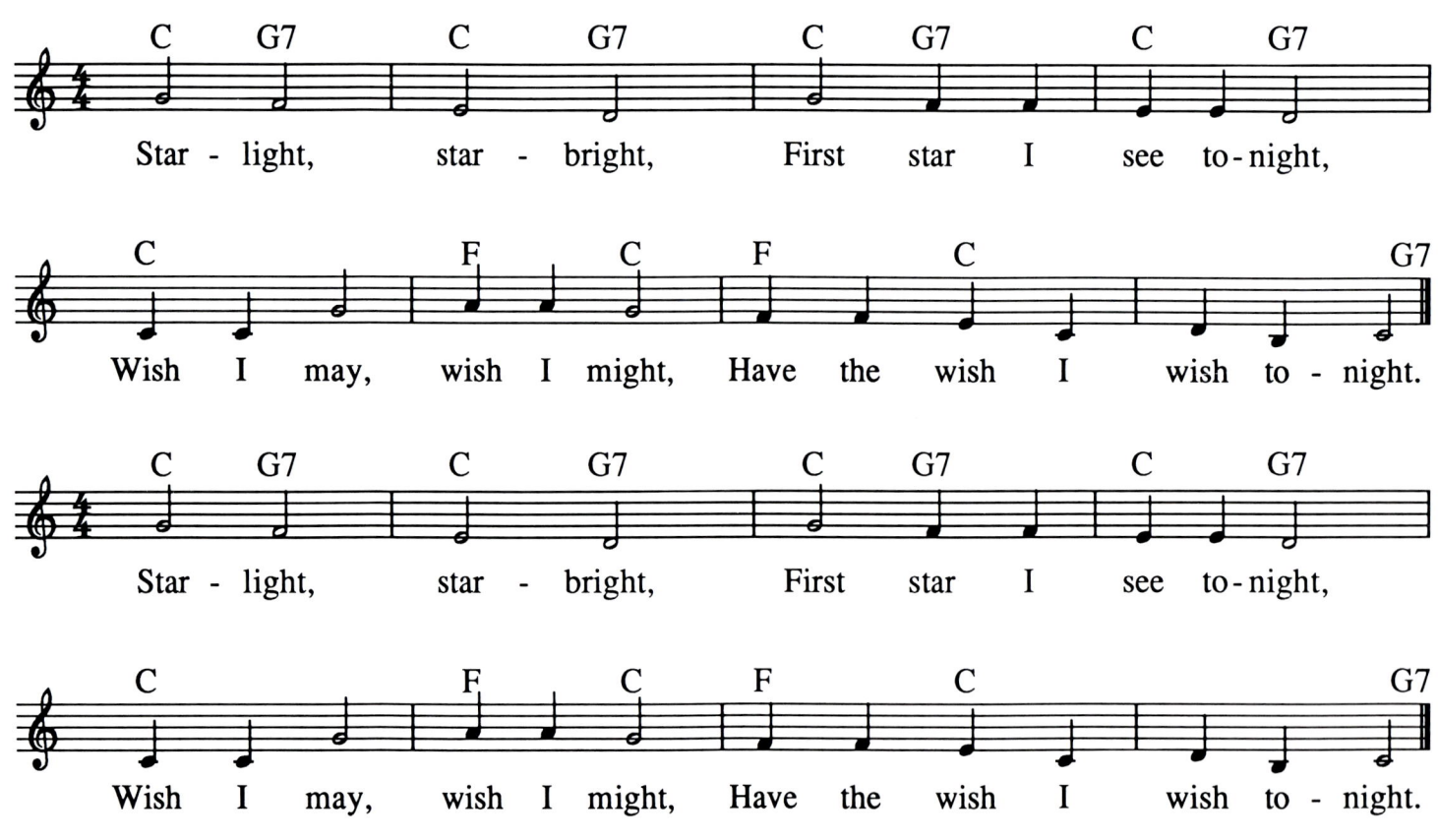

All Through the Night
Welsh

Sleep, my child, and peace attend thee
All through the night;
Guardian angels God will send thee
All through the night.
Soft the drowsy hours are creeping,
Hill and vale in slumber sleeping,
I my loving vigil keeping
All through the night.

While the moon her watch is keeping
All through the night;
While the weary world is sleeping
All through the night.
O'er thy spirit gently stealing,
Visions of delight revealing,
Breathes a pure and holy feeling
All through the night.

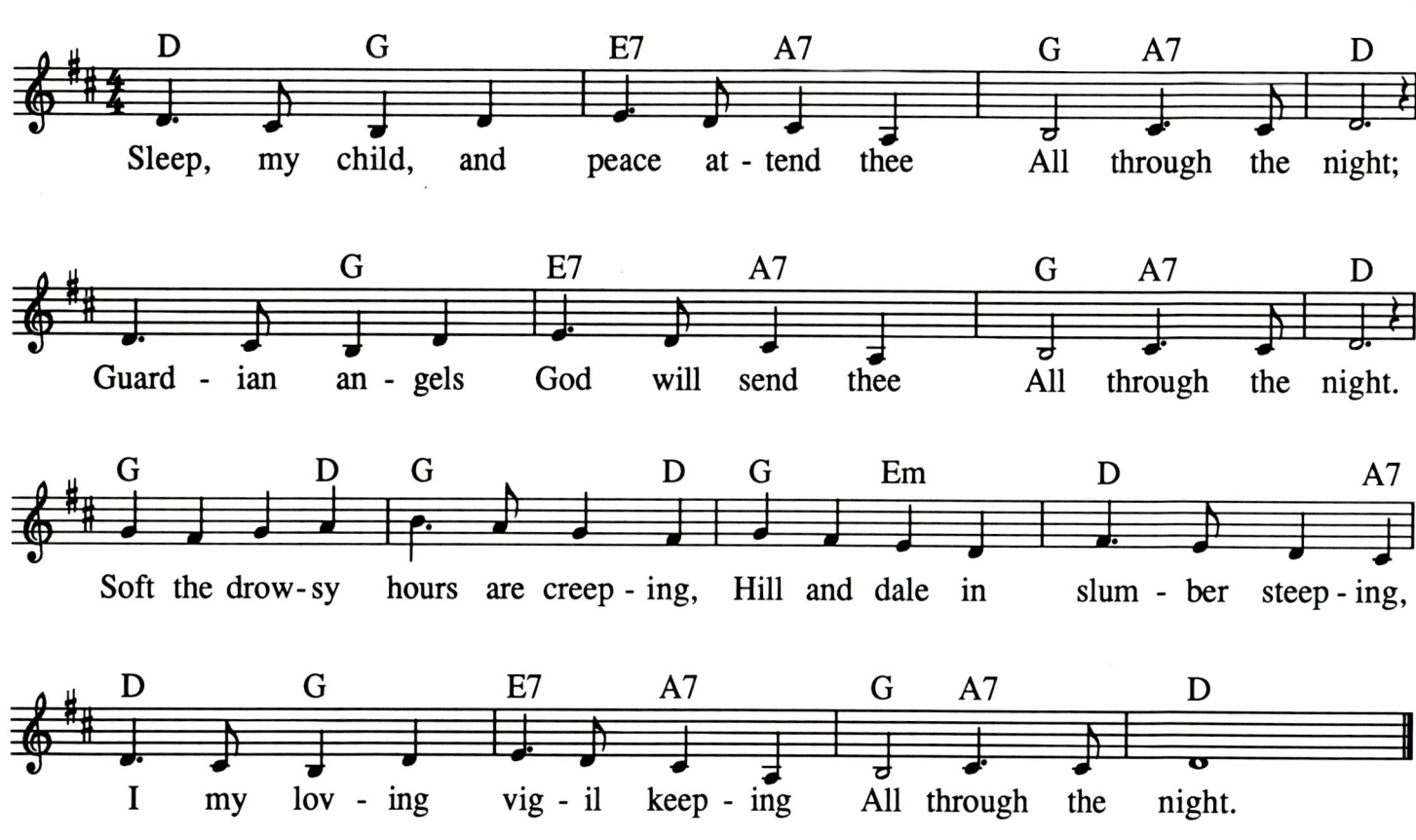

Golden Slumbers
English

Golden slumbers kiss your eyes,
Smiles awake you when you rise;
Sleep, pretty darling, do not cry,
And I will sing a lullaby.

Care you know not, therefore sleep,
While over you our watch we keep;
Sleep, pretty darling, do not cry,
And I will sing a lullaby.

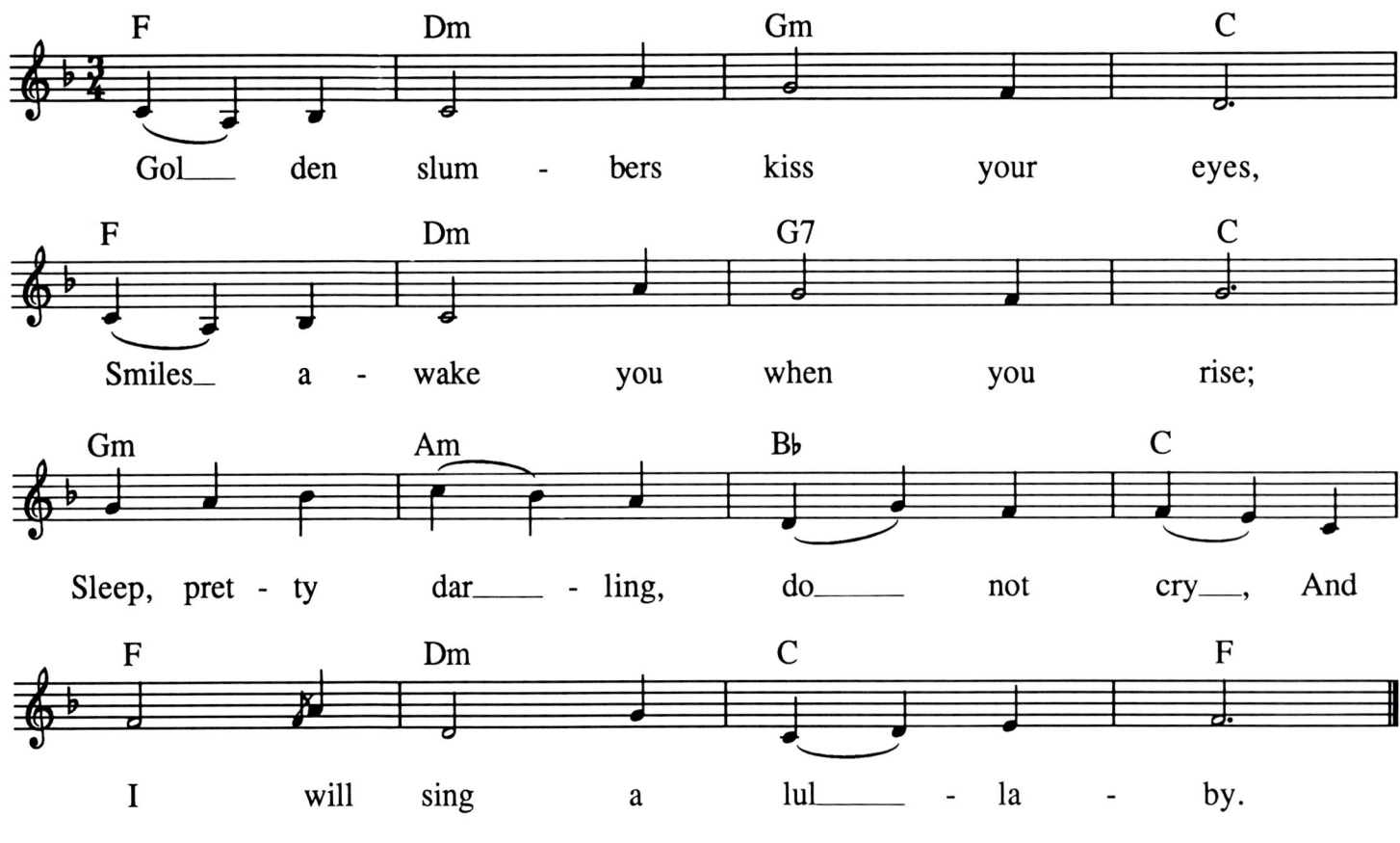

Wee Willie Winkie
Scottish

Wee Willie Winkie
Runs through the town,
Upstairs and downstairs,
In his nightgown.

Rapping at the window,
Crying at the lock,
'Are the children in their beds?
For it's past eight o'clock'.

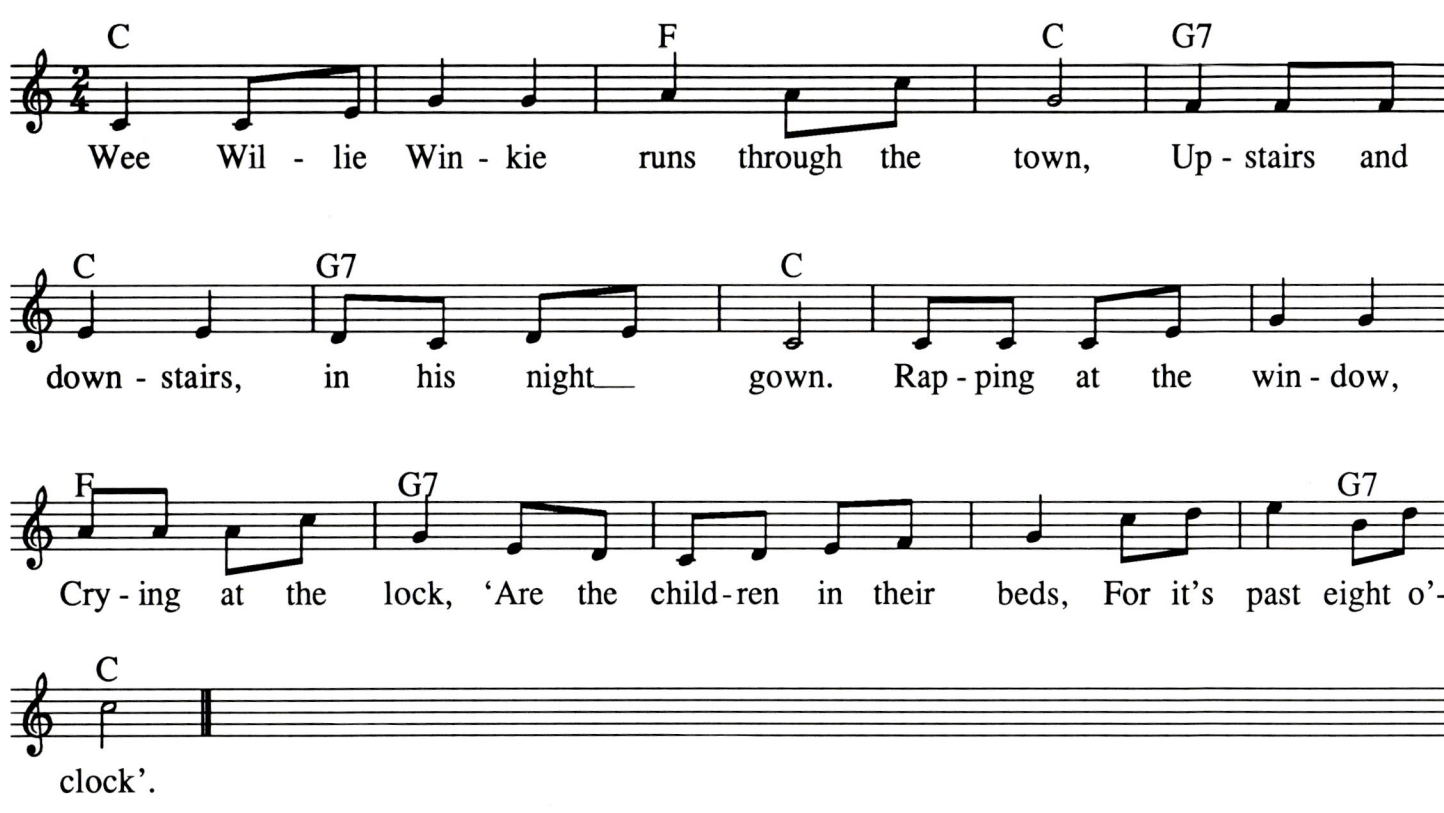

Cradle Song
German

Slumber, slumber, o my darling baby,
Gently rocked by mother's loving arm.
Safely rest and softly slumber,
And her love shall shelter you from harm.

Slumber, slumber in your cradle swinging,
Rocking gently, by your mother's hand.
Peaceful slumber rest is bringing,
Dreams shall send you on to Slumberland.

Schlafe, schlafe, holder süßer Knabe,
Leise wiegt dich deiner Mutter Hand;
Sanfte Ruhe, milde Labe
Bringt dir schwebend dieses Wiegenband.

Schlafe, schlafe, in dem süßen Grabe,
Noch beschützt dich deiner Mutter Arm;
Alle Wünsche, alle Habe
Faßt sie liebend, alle liebewarm.

When the Night-time Comes
Polish

When the night-time comes so darkly,
With its starry apron high,
Little birds peep out with their bright eyes
At the stars that blink and shine.

From their nests they gaze in awe,
Little sleepy heads no more;
And they cheeped and chirped and they sighed
For a star to call their own.

Mother said, 'Let the night not see you,
For the stars are not to keep,
And the old grey cat may hear you,
Hush-a-bye, it's time to sleep.'

Idzie niebo ciemną nocą,
Ma w fartuszku pełno gwiazd;
Gwiazdy błyszczą i migocą
Aż wyjrzały ptaszki z gniazd.

Jak wyjrzały, zobaczyły,
To nie chciały wcale spać;
Kaprysiły, grymasiły,
Żeby im po jednej dać.

Gwiazdki nie są do zabawy,
Toż by nocka była zła.
Bo usłyszy kot kulawy,
Cicho bądźcie! Aaa.

Bye, Baby Bunting
English

Bye, baby Bunting,
Daddy's gone a-hunting
To catch a little rabbit skin
To wrap my baby Bunting in.

Bye, baby Bunting,
Daddy's gone a-hunting
To catch a little rabbit skin
To wrap my baby Bunting in.

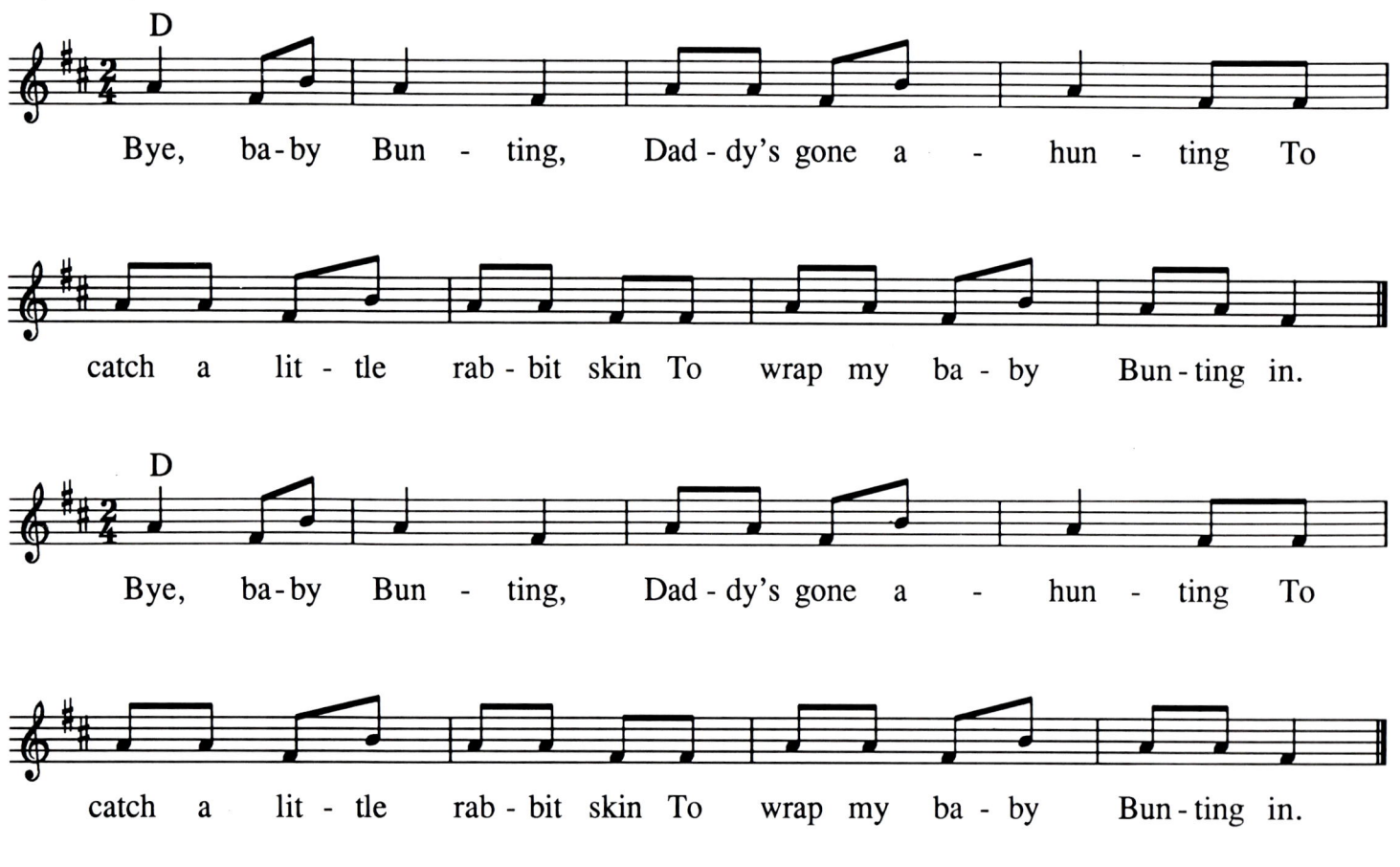

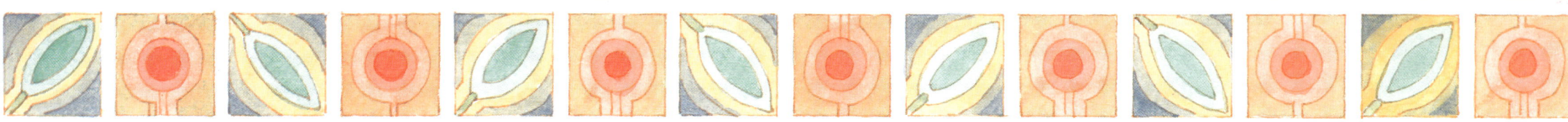

Maranoa Lullaby
Australian (Aboriginal)

By the firelight,   Mumma warrunno
In the dark of night,   Murra wathunno
Child against my breast,   Mumma warrunno
Safely you shall rest.   Murra wathunno

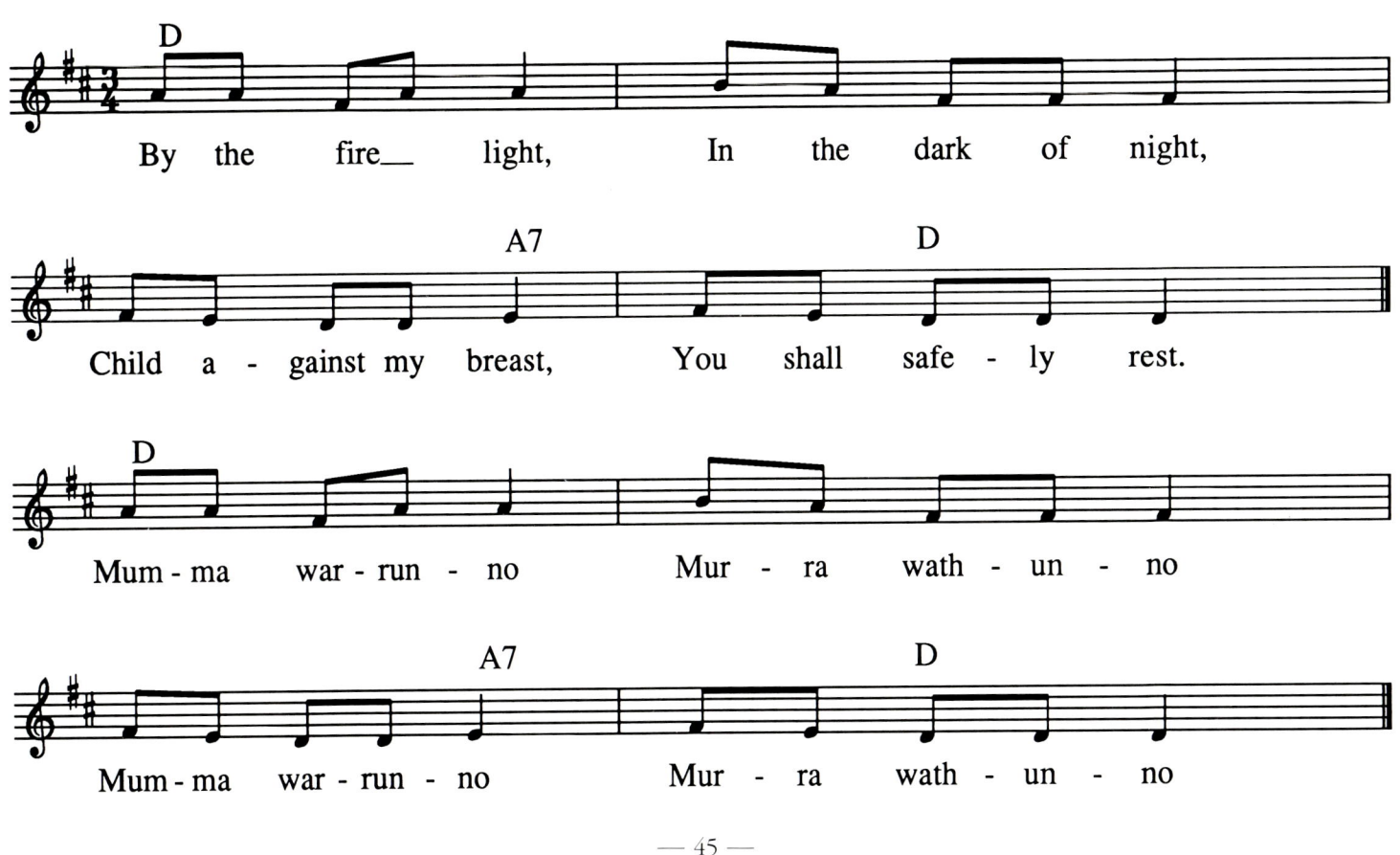

Sleep, Baby, Sleep!
Dutch

Sleep, baby, sleep!
Outside there walks a sheep:
A sheep with little white feet,
Who drinks his milk so sweet.

Sleep, baby, sleep,
Outside there walks a sheep.

Slaap, kindje, slaap!
Daar buiten loopt een schaap:
Een schaap met witte voetjes,
Dat drinkt zijn melk zo zoetjes.

Slaap, kindje, slaap,
Daar buiten loopt een schaap.

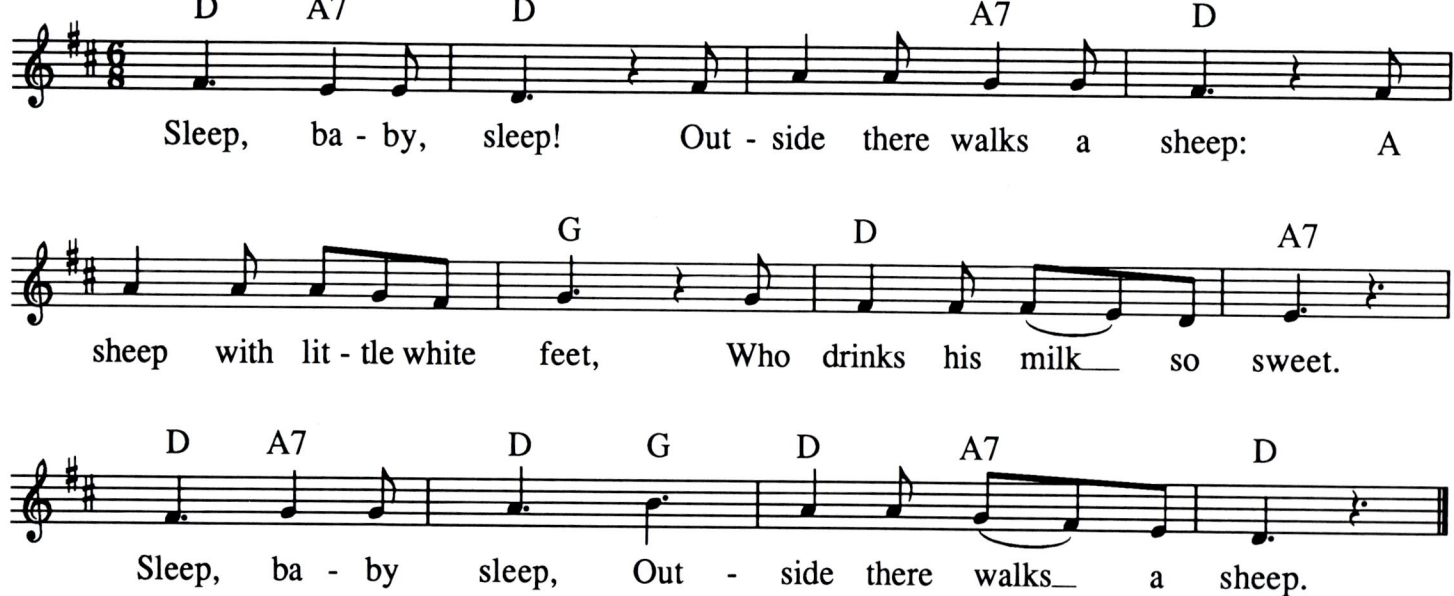

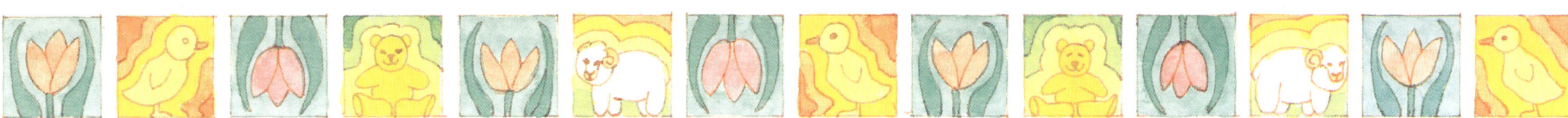

Lullaby, My Baby
Spanish

Lullaby, my baby,	Arroro mi niño,
Lullaby, my sun,	Arroro mi sol,
Little part of my heart,	Duérmase pedazo,
Sleep now little one.	De mi corazón.

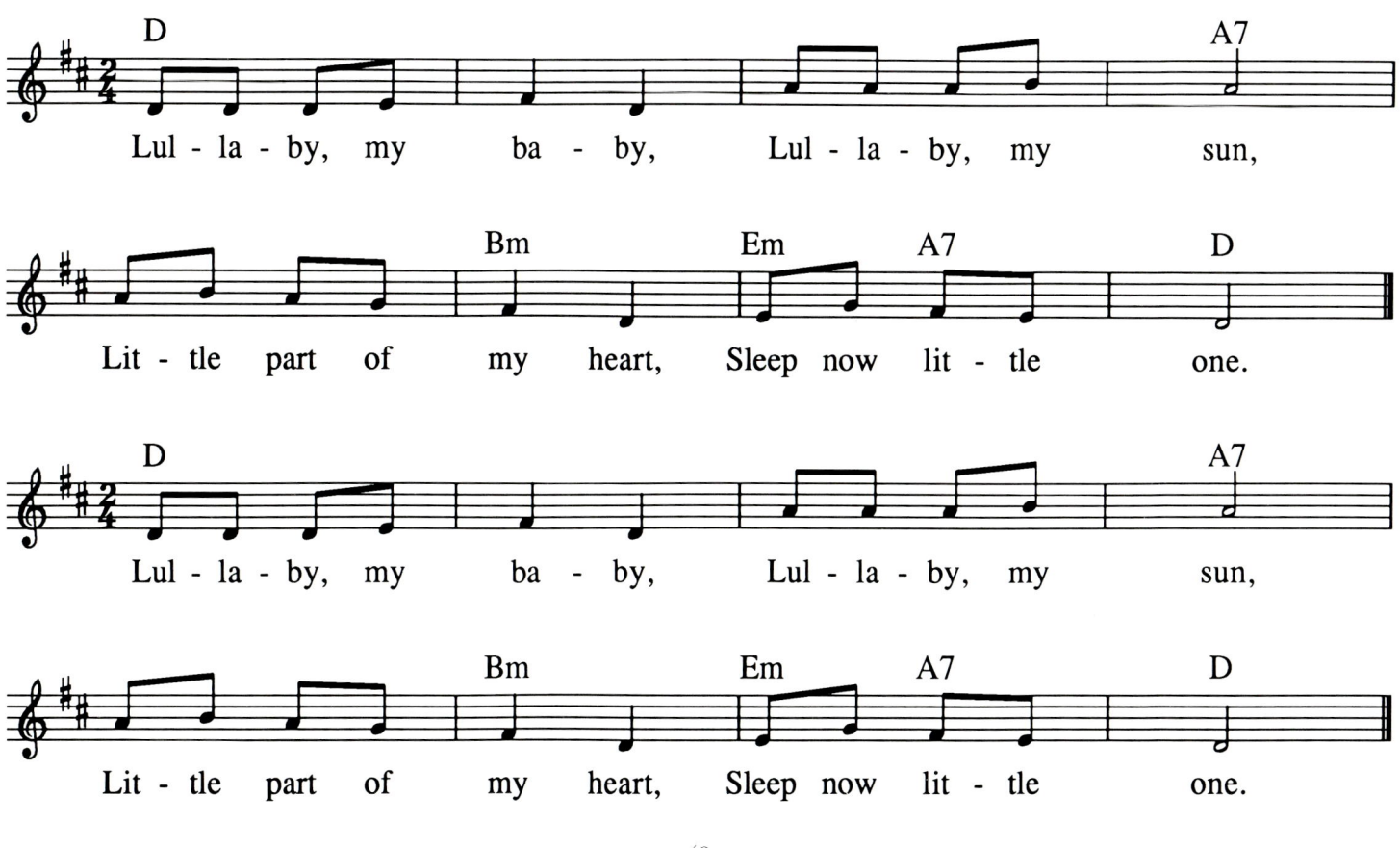

Baloo Baleerie
Scottish

Baloo baleerie, baloo baleerie,
Baloo baleerie, baloo balee.

Go away, little fairies,   Gang awa' neerie fairies,
Go away, little fairies,   Gang awa' neerie fairies,
Go away, little fairies,   Gang awa' neerie fairies,
From our small room.   Frae oor ben noo.

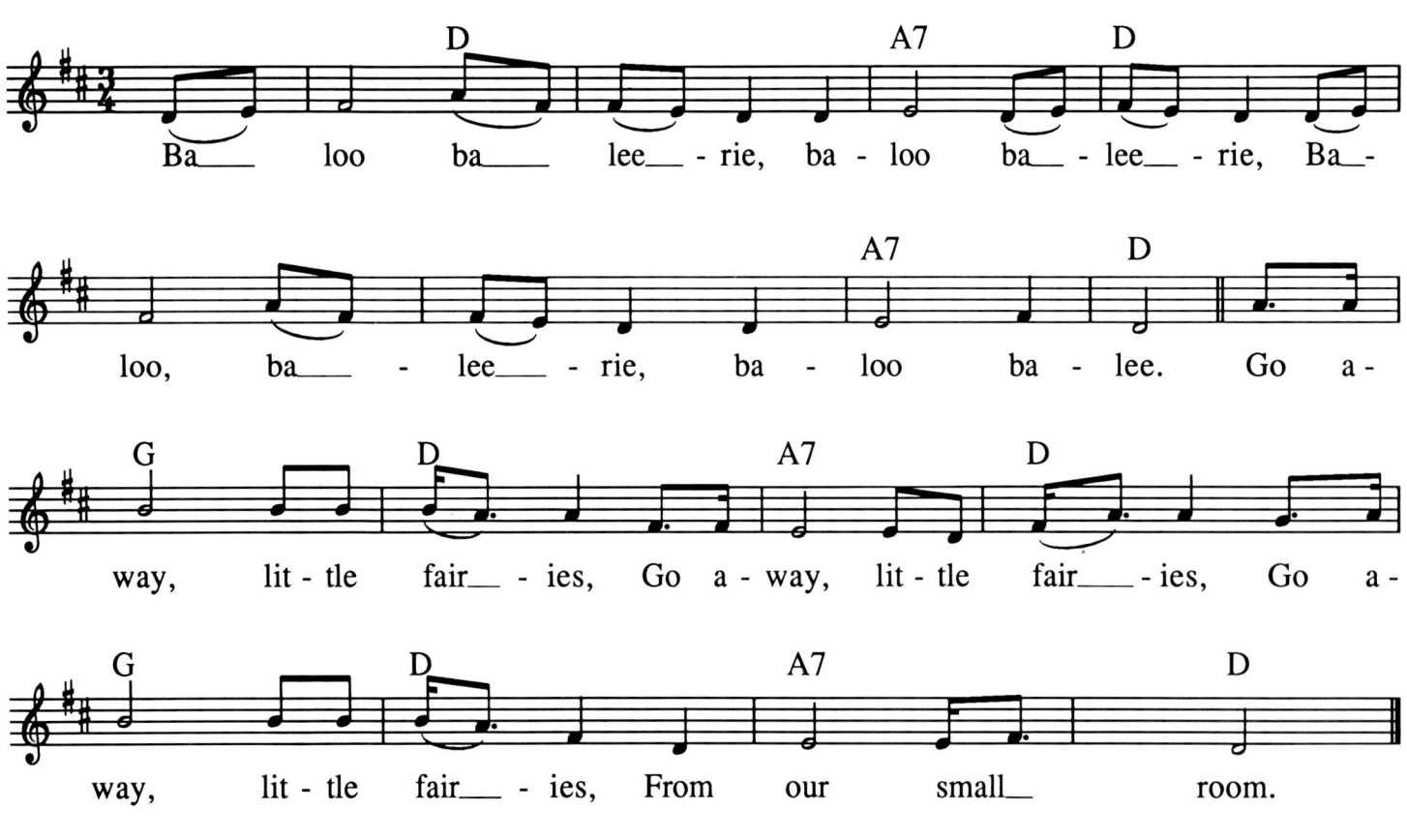

Information about the lullabies

All songs have been collected, scored and adapted by Mark Leehy and Kevin O'Mara © 1992.

Brahms Lullaby *German*
Known under different titles and with an endless supply of translations, the original tune is by Johannes Brahms, with lyrics by his friend Fritz Simrock. We have attempted a composite version of the English words.

Kumbayah *West Indian*
This black American spiritual, 'Come by here, my Lord', travelled the slave routes to the West Indies and returned to America as a dialect lullaby. By changing one word each time, endless verses may be created.

Twinkle, Twinkle, Little Star *English*
First appearing as a much longer poem in 1806, this eternal piece was written by Jane and Ann Taylor, and is commonly set to an old French tune.

Nursemaid's Lullaby *Japanese*
Impoverished Japanese families commonly sent a younger daughter to babysit for the wealthy. This song is a little sad, as the girl longs for time to play like other children.

Hush, Little Baby
American (North Carolina)
This famous song has as many versions as it has singers, and has even been a 'hit' rock song. Also known as 'Mockingbird', it comes from South Carolina, but harks back to a much older English tradition of riddle songs.

Au Clair de la Lune *French*
This beautiful song is familiar to most French children, but the true significance of Pierrot's late-night visit may never be known.

Ninna Nanna *Italian*
Every Italian region has its own, very different, version of this song. Our adaptation is a distillation of our favourites.

All the Pretty Little Horses
The American South
An American song that may have had its beginnings as a sad protest, sung by a black woman, rocking the master's baby.

Hine E Hine *New Zealand (Maori)*
Written by Te Range Pai, this is a rare example of a father taking on the duties of singing a daughter to sleep.

Sleep, O Babe *Irish*
In this mystical Irish lullaby, rich in symbol and myth, the mother sings to protect her child from the faeries and 'other world' beings that might take her child.

Hush-a-bye, Baby *English*
Also known as 'Rock-a-bye, Baby', this classic lullaby may have originated as a parody, written by one of the Mayflower Pilgrims, on the American Indian practice of suspending bark 'cradles' from low branches.

Bayushka Baio *Russian*
Also known as 'Babushka Baiou, this haunting song is common in Russia and surrounding countries. It may come from 'bayukat' meaning 'to lull', or from 'babushka', meaning 'grandmother'.

Starlight, Starbright *English*
We have adapted the tune of this old English poem from many different versions.

All Through the Night *Welsh*
The original words, 'Ar Hyd y Nos' were written by Sir Harold Boulton in 1884, and have been tinkered with ever since. Now it's our turn! The tune is a very old Welsh air.

Golden Slumbers *English*
Written by Thomas Dekker in 1603, in a longer and slightly different version. Our tune is one of several different melodies commonly used.

Wee Willie Winkie *Scottish*
Written by William Miller in 1841, in a much longer and more 'Scottish' version, this song appears here as an adaptation of its more common settings.

Cradle Song *German*
The beautiful tune from Germany, and our words are adapted from many different sets of verses.

When the Night-time Comes *Polish*
A 'cautionary' song from Poland, this delightful lullaby is basically saying that mother knows best.

Bye, Baby Bunting *English*
A universal lullaby from England. 'Bunting' could refer to festive decoration, or it could be a term of endearment towards the baby.

Maranoa Lullaby
Australian (Aboriginal)
A Murri song from the Aborigines of Queensland, collected by Dr H.O. Lethbridge. No translation can ever be accurate, so we have attempted to capture the spirit of the song with our own words.

Sleep, Baby, Sleep! *Dutch*
A Dutch lullaby, 'Sláap, Kindje, Slaap' that follows a European pastoral tradition. It is a close relative of the German 'Schlaf, Kindlein, Schlaf'.

Lullaby, My Baby *Spanish*
A simple and charming song from Spain.

Baloo Baleerie *Scottish*
A Gaelic lullaby, where the 'Ben' refers to the nursery.